The Key Facts™ on

Kyrgyzstan

Essential Information on Kyrgyzstan

By Patrick W. Nee

The Internationalist®

www.internationalist.com

The Internationalist®

International Business, Investment, and Travel

Published by:

The Internationalist Publishing Company

96 Walter Street/ Suite 200

Boston, MA 02131, USA

Tel: 617-354-7722

www.internationalist.com

PN@internationalist.com

Table Of Contents

Chapter 1: Background

A Central Asian country of incredible natural beauty and proud nomadic traditions, most of Kyrgyzstan was formally annexed to Russia in 1876. The Kyrgyz staged a major revolt against the Tsarist Empire in 1916 in which almost one-sixth of the Kyrgyz population was killed. Kyrgyzstan became a Soviet republic in 1936 and achieved independence in 1991 when the USSR dissolved. Nationwide demonstrations in the spring of 2005 resulted in the ouster of President Askar AKAEV, who had run the country since 1990. Former prime minister Kurmanbek BAKIEV overwhelmingly won the presidential election in the summer of 2005. Over the next few years, he manipulated the parliament to accrue new powers for the presidency. In July 2009, after months of harassment against his opponents and media critics, BAKIEV won re-election in a presidential campaign that the international community deemed flawed. In April 2010, violent protests in Bishkek led to the collapse of the BAKIEV regime and his eventual fleeing to Minsk, Belarus. His successor, Roza OTUNBAEVA, served as transitional president until Almazbek ATAMBAEV was inaugurated in December 2011, marking the first peaceful transfer of presidential power in independent Kyrgyzstan's history. Continuing concerns include: the trajectory of democratization, endemic corruption, poor interethnic relations, and terrorism.

Chapter 2: Geography

Location:

Central Asia, west of China, south of Kazakhstan

Geographic coordinates:

41 00 N, 75 00 E

Map references:

Asia

Area:

total: 199,951 sq km

country comparison to the world: 87

land: 191,801 sq km

water: 8,150 sq km

Area - comparative:

slightly smaller than South Dakota

Land boundaries:

total: 3,051 km

border countries: China 858 km, Kazakhstan 1,224 km,

Tajikistan 870 km, Uzbekistan 1,099 km

Coastline:

0 km (landlocked)

Maritime claims:

none (landlocked)

Climate:

dry continental to polar in high Tien Shan Mountains; subtropical in southwest (Fergana Valley); temperate in northern foothill zone

Terrain:

peaks of Tien Shan and associated valleys and basins encompass entire nation

Elevation extremes:

lowest point: Kara-Daryya (Karadar'ya) 132 m

highest point: Jengish Chokusu (Pik Pobedy) 7,439 m

Natural resources:

abundant hydropower; significant deposits of gold and rare earth metals; locally exploitable coal, oil, and natural gas; other deposits of nepheline, mercury, bismuth, lead, and zinc

Land use:

arable land: 6.38%

permanent crops: 0.37%

other: 93.24%

note: Kyrgyzstan has the world's largest natural-growth walnut forest (2011)

Irrigated land:

10,210 sq km (2005)

Total renewable water resources:

23.62 cu km (2011)

Freshwater withdrawal (domestic/industrial/agricultural):

total: 8.01 cu km/yr (3%/4%/93%)

per capita: 1,558 cu m/yr (2006)

Natural hazards:

NA

Environment - current issues:

water pollution; many people get their water directly from contaminated streams and wells; as a result, water-borne diseases are prevalent; increasing soil salinity from faulty irrigation practices

Environment - international agreements:

party to: Air Pollution, Biodiversity, Climate Change, Climate Change-Kyoto Protocol, Desertification, Hazardous Wastes, Ozone Layer Protection, Wetlands signed, but not ratified: none of the selected agreements

Geography - note:

landlocked; entirely mountainous, dominated by the Tien Shan range; 94% of the country is 1,000 m above sea level with an average elevation of 2,750 m; many tall peaks, glaciers, and high-altitude lakes

Chapter 3: People and Society

Nationality:

> noun: Kyrgyzstani(s)

> adjective: Kyrgyzstani

Ethnic groups:

> Kyrgyz 64.9%, Uzbek 13.8%, Russian 12.5%, Dungan 1.1%, Ukrainian 1%, Uighur 1%, other 5.7% (1999 census)

Languages:

> Kyrgyz (official) 64.7%, Uzbek 13.6%, Russian (official) 12.5%, Dungun 1%, other 8.2% (1999 census)

Religions:

> Muslim 75%, Russian Orthodox 20%, other 5%

Population:

> 5,604,212 (July 2014 est.)

> country comparison to the world: 114

Age structure:

> 0-14 years: 29.8% (male 854,029/female 815,300)

> 15-24 years: 18.8% (male 536,355/female 519,440)

> 25-54 years: 39.4% (male 1,079,691/female 1,127,520)

> 55-64 years: 4.9% (male 171,960/female 224,450)

> 65 years and over: 4.9% (male 105,651/female 169,816) (2014 est.)

Dependency ratios:

    total dependency ratio: 52.7 %

    youth dependency ratio: 46.4 %

    elderly dependency ratio: 6.4 %

    potential support ratio: 15.7 (2013)

Median age:

    total: 25.7 years

    male: 24.7 years

    female: 26.7 years (2014 est.)

Population growth rate:

    1.04% (2014 est.)

    country comparison to the world: 115

Birth rate:

    23.33 births/1,000 population (2014 est.)

    country comparison to the world: 69

Death rate:

    6.74 deaths/1,000 population (2014 est.)

    country comparison to the world: 142

Net migration rate:

    -6.16 migrant(s)/1,000 population (2014 est.)

    country comparison to the world: 199

Urbanization:

    urban population: 35.3% of total population (2011)

    rate of urbanization: 1.31% annual rate of change (2010-15 est.)

Major urban areas - population:

BISHKEK (capital) 854,000 (2009)

Sex ratio:

at birth: 1.07 male(s)/female

0-14 years: 1.05 male(s)/female

15-24 years: 1.03 male(s)/female

25-54 years: 0.96 male(s)/female

55-64 years: 0.96 male(s)/female

65 years and over: 0.63 male(s)/female

total population: 0.96 male(s)/female (2014 est.)

Mother's mean age at first birth:

23.6 (2010 est.)

Maternal mortality rate:

71 deaths/100,000 live births (2010)

country comparison to the world: 86

Infant mortality rate:

total: 28.71 deaths/1,000 live births

country comparison to the world: 67

male: 32.98 deaths/1,000 live births

female: 24.16 deaths/1,000 live births (2014 est.)

Life expectancy at birth:

total population: 70.06 years

country comparison to the world: 153

male: 65.89 years

female: 74.51 years (2014 est.)

Total fertility rate:

> 2.68 children born/woman (2014 est.)

> country comparison to the world: 73

Contraceptive prevalence rate:

> 47.8% (2005/06)

Health expenditures:

> 6.2% of GDP (2010)

> country comparison to the world: 102

Physicians density:

> 2.47 physicians/1,000 population (2011)

Hospital bed density:

> 4.8 beds/1,000 population (2011)

Drinking water source:

> improved:

>> *urban*: 96% of population

>> *rural*: 84.7% of population

>> *total*: 88.7% of population

> unimproved:

>> *urban*: 4% of population

>> *rural*: 15.3% of population

>> *total*: 11.3% of population (2011 est.)

Sanitation facility access:

> improved:

>> *urban*: 93.6% of population

>> *rural*: 93.1% of population

>> *total*: 93.3% of population

unimproved:

> *urban*: 6.4% of population
>
> *rural*: 6.9% of population
>
> *total*: 6.7% of population (2011 est.)

HIV/AIDS - adult prevalence rate:

> 0.3% (2012)
>
> country comparison to the world: 95

HIV/AIDS - people living with HIV/AIDS:

> 8,700 (2012)
>
> country comparison to the world: 108

HIV/AIDS - deaths:

> 300 (2012)
>
> country comparison to the world: 102

Obesity - adult prevalence rate:

> 15.5% (2008)
>
> country comparison to the world: 118

Children under the age of 5 underweight:

> 2.7% (2006)
>
> country comparison to the world: 116

Education expenditures:

> 6.8% of GDP (2011)
>
> country comparison to the world: 25

Literacy:

definition: age 15 and over can read and write

total population: 99.2%

male: 99.5%

female: 99% (2009 est.)

School life expectancy (primary to tertiary education):

total: 13 years

male: 12 years

female: 13 years (2011)

Child labor – children ages 5-14:

total number: 563,920

percentage: 40.3 %

note: data represents children ages 5-17 (2007 est.)

Unemployment, youth ages 15-24:

total: 14.6%

country comparison to the world: 86

male: 13.6%

female: 16.2% (2006)

Chapter 4: Government and Key Leaders

Country name:

> conventional long form: Kyrgyz Republic
>
> conventional short form: Kyrgyzstan
>
> local long form: Kyrgyz Respublikasy
>
> local short form: Kyrgyzstan
>
> former: Kirghiz Soviet Socialist Republic

Government type:

> republic

Capital:

> name: Bishkek
>
> geographic coordinates: 42 52 N, 74 36 E
>
> time difference: UTC+6 (11 hours ahead of Washington, DC during Standard Time)

Administrative divisions:

> 7 provinces (oblustar, singular - oblus) and 2 cities* (shaarlar, singular - shaar); Batken Oblusu, Bishkek Shaary*, Chuy Oblusu (Bishkek), Jalal-Abad Oblusu, Naryn Oblusu, Osh Oblusu, Osh Shaary*, Talas Oblusu, Ysyk-Kol Oblusu (Karakol)
>
> note: administrative divisions have the same names as their administrative centers (exceptions have the administrative center name following in parentheses)

Independence:

> 31 August 1991 (from the Soviet Union)

National holiday:

Independence Day, 31 August (1991)

Constitution:

previous 1993; latest adopted 27 June 2010, effective 2 July 2010 (2010)

Legal system:

civil law system which includes features of French civil law and Russian Federation laws

International law organization participation:

has not submitted an ICJ jurisdiction declaration; non-party state to the ICCt

Suffrage:

18 years of age; universal

Executive branch:

chief of state: President Almazbek ATAMBAEV (since 1 December 2011)

head of government: Prime Minister Joomart OTORBAEV (since 2 April 2014, acting since 26 March 2014); First Deputy Prime Minister - Tayyrbek SARPASHEV (since 2 April 2014); Deputy Prime Ministers - Valeriy DIL, Abdyrakhman MAMATALIEV, Elvira SARIEVA (all since 2 April 2014)

cabinet: Cabinet of Ministers proposed by the prime minister, appointed by the president; ministers in charge of defense and security are appointed solely by the president electionspresident elected by popular vote for one six-year term; election last held on 30 October 2011 (next to be held in 2017); prime minister nominated by the parliamentary party holding more than 50% of the seats; if no such party exists, the president selects the party that will form a coalition majority and government

election results: Almazbek ATAMBAEV elected president; percent of vote - Almazbek ATAMBAEV 63.2%, Adakhan MADUMAROV 14.7%, Kamchybek TASHIEV 14.3%, other 7.8%; Jantoro SATYBALDIEV elected prime minister; parliamentary vote - 111-2

Legislative branch:

unicameral Supreme Council or Jogorku Kengesh (120 seats; members elected by popular vote to serve five-year terms)

elections: last held on 10 October 2010 (next to be held in 2015)

election results: Supreme Council - percent of vote by party - NA; seats by party - Ata-Jurt 28, SDPK 26, Ar-Namys 25, Respublika 23, Ata-Meken 18

Judicial branch:

Highest court(s): Supreme Court (consists of 25 judges); Constitutional Court (consists of 9 judges)

<u>Judge selection and term of offfice:</u> Supreme Court and Constitutional Court judges appointed by the Supreme Council on the recommendation of the president; Supreme Court judges serve for 10 years, Constitutional Court judges serve for 15 years; mandatory retirement at age 70 for judges of both courts

<u>subordinate courts:</u> Higher Court of Arbitration; oblast (provincial) and city courts

Political parties and leaders:

Ar-Namys (Dignity) Party [Feliks KULOV]

Ata-Jurt (Homeland) [Kamchybek TASHIEV, Akhmat KELDIBEKOV, Sadyr JAPAROV]

Ata-Meken (Fatherland) [Omurbek TEKEBAEV]

Butun Kyrgyzstan (All Kyrgyzstan) [Adakhan MADUMAROV]

Respublika [Omurbek BABANOV]

Social-Democratic Party of Kyrgyzstan (SDPK) [Almazbek ATAMBAEV]

Political pressure groups and leaders:

Adilet (Justice) Legal Clinic [Cholpon JAKUPOVA]

Citizens Against Corruption [Tolekan ISMAILOVA]

Coalition for Democracy and Civil Society [Dinara OSHURAKHUNOVA]

Kylym Shamy (Torch of the Century) [Aziza ABDIRASULOVA]

Precedent Partnership Group [Nurbek
TOKTAKUNOV]
Societal Analysis Public Association [Rita
KARASARTOVA]
Union of True Muslims [Nurlan MOTUEV]

International organization participation:

ADB, CICA, CIS, CSTO, EAEC, EAPC, EBRD, ECO,
EITI (compliant country), FAO, GCTU, IAEA, IBRD,
ICAO, ICC (NGOs), ICRM, IDA, IDB, IFAD, IFC,
IFRCS, ILO, IMF, Interpol, IOC, IOM, IPU, ISO
(correspondent), ITSO, ITU, MIGA, NAM (observer),
OIC, OPCW, OSCE, PCA, PFP, SCO, UN, UNCTAD,
UNESCO, UNIDO, UNISFA, UNMIL, UNMISS,
UNWTO, UPU, WCO, WFTU (NGOs), WHO, WIPO,
WMO, WTO

Diplomatic representation in the US:

chief of mission: Ambassador Mukhtar JUMALIEV (since
7 December 2010)
chancery: 2360 Massachusetts Ave. NW, Washington, DC
20008
telephone: [1] (202) 449-9822
FAX: [1] (202) 386-7550
consulate(s) general: New York

Diplomatic representation from the US:

chief of mission: Ambassador Pamela L. SPRATLEN
(since 15 April 2011)

embassy: 171 Prospect Mira, Bishkek 720016

mailing address: use embassy street address

telephone: [996] (312) 551-241, (517) 777-217

FAX: [996] (312) 551-264

Key Leaders:

Pres.	Almazbek ATAMBAEV
Prime Min.	Joomart OTORBAEV
First Dep. Prime Min.	Tayyrbek SARPASHEV
Dep. Prime Min.	Valeriy DIL
Dep. Prime Min.	Abdyrakhman MAMATALIEV
Dep. Prime Min.	Elvira SARIEVA
Min. & Chief of the Govt. Apparatus	Nurkhanbek MOMUNALIEV
Min. of Agriculture & Water Management	Taalaybek AYDARALIEV
Min. of Culture, Tourism, & Information	Kamila TALIEVA
Min. of Defense	Abibula KUDAYBERDIEV, *Maj. Gen.*
Min. of Economy & Antimonopoly Policies	Temir SARIEV
Min. of Education & Science	Kanatbek SADYKOV
Min. of Emergency Situations	Kubatbek BORONOV
Min. of Energy & Industry	Osmonbek ARTYKBAEV
Min. of Finance	Olga LAVROVA
Min. of Foreign Affairs	Erlan ABDYLDAEV
Min. of Health Care	Dinara SAGINBAEVA

Min. of Internal Affairs	Abdylda SURANCHIEV
Min. of Justice	Almambet SHYKMAMATOV
Min. of Labor, Migration, & Youth	Aliyasbek ALYMKULOV
Min. of Social Development	Kudaybergen BAZARBAEV
Min. of Transportation & Communication	Kalykbek SULTANOV
Chmn., State Ctte. for National Security (GKNB)	Busurmankul TABALDIEV
Prosecutor Gen.	Aida SALYANOVA
Chmn., National Bank of Kyrgyzstan	Zina ASANKOJOEVA
Ambassador to the US	Mukhtar JUMALIEV
Permanent Representative to the UN, New York	Taalaybek KYDYROV

Flag description:

red field with a yellow sun in the center having 40 rays representing the 40 Kyrgyz tribes; on the obverse side the rays run counterclockwise, on the reverse, clockwise; in the center of the sun is a red ring crossed by two sets of three lines, a stylized representation of a "tunduk" - the crown of a traditional Kyrgyz yurt; red symbolizes bravery and valor, the sun evinces peace and wealth

National symbol(s):

gyrfalcon

National anthem:

name: "Kyrgyz Respublikasynyn Mamlekettik Gimni" (National Anthem of the Kyrgyz Republic)

lyrics/music: Djamil SADYKOV and Eshmambet
KULUEV/Nasyr DAVLESOV and Kalyi
MOLDOBASANOV
<u>note</u>: adopted 1992

Chapter 5: Economy

Economy - overview:

Kyrgyzstan is a poor, mountainous country with a dominant agricultural sector. Cotton, tobacco, wool, and meat are the main agricultural products, although only tobacco and cotton are exported in any quantity. Industrial exports include gold, mercury, uranium, natural gas, and electricity. The economy depends heavily on gold exports - mainly from output at the Kumtor gold mine - and on remittances from Kyrgyzstani migrant workers primarily in Russia. Following independence, Kyrgyzstan was progressive in carrying out market reforms, such as an improved regulatory system and land reform. Kyrgyzstan was the first Commonwealth of Independent States (CIS) country to be accepted into the World Trade Organization. Much of the government's stock in enterprises has been sold. Drops in production had been severe after the breakup of the Soviet Union in December 1991, but by mid-1995, production began to recover and exports began to increase. The overthrow of President BAKIEV in April 2010 and subsequent ethnic clashes left hundreds dead and damaged infrastructure. Under President ATAMBAYEV, Kyrgyzstan has developed a plan for economic development in coordination with international donors, and has also expressed its intent to join the Customs Union of Russia, Belarus, and Kazakhstan. Progress in fighting corruption, improving transparency in licensing, business permits and taxations, restructuring domestic industry, and attracting foreign aid and investment are key to future growth.

GDP (purchasing power parity):

$14.3 billion (2013 est.)

country comparison to the world: 145

$13.32 billion (2012 est.)

$13.44 billion (2011 est.)

note: data are in 2013 US dollars

GDP (official exchange rate):

$7.234 billion (2013 est.)

GDP - real growth rate:

7.4% (2013 est.)

country comparison to the world: 17

-0.9% (2012 est.)

6% (2011 est.)

GDP - per capita (PPP):

$2,500 (2013 est.)

country comparison to the world: 185

$2,400 (2012 est.)

$2,400 (2011 est.)

note: data are in 2013 US dollars

Gross national saving:

9.1% of GDP (2013 est.)

country comparison to the world: 140

2.4% of GDP (2012 est.)

15% of GDP (2011 est.)

GDP – composition, by end use:

household consumption: 78.1%

government consumption: 17.6%

investment in fixed capital: 25.3%

investment in inventories: 8%

exports of goods and services: 51.2%

imports of goods and services: -80.2%

GDP - composition by sector:

agriculture: 20.8%

industry: 34.4%

services: 44.8% (2013 est.)

Agriculture – products:

tobacco, cotton, potatoes, vegetables, grapes, fruits and berries; sheep, goats, cattle, wool

Industries:

small machinery, textiles, food processing, cement, shoes, sawn logs, refrigerators, furniture, electric motors, gold, rare earth metals

Industrial production growth rate:

12% (2013 est.)

country comparison to the world: 6

Labor force:

2.344 million (2007)

country comparison to the world: 115

Labor force - by occupation:

agriculture: 48%

industry: 12.5%

services: 39.5% (2005 est.)

Unemployment rate:

8.6% (2011 est.)

country comparison to the world: 95

18% (2004 est.)

Population below poverty line:

33.7% (2011 est.)

Household income or consumption by percentage share:

lowest 10%: 2.8%

highest 10%: 27.8% (2009 est.)

Distribution of family income - Gini index:

33.4 (2007)

country comparison to the world: 98

29 (2001)

Budget:

revenues: $2.128 billion

expenditures: $2.458 billion (2013 est.)

Taxes and other revenues:

29.4% of GDP (2013 est.)

country comparison to the world: 94

Budget surplus (+) or deficit (-):

-4.6% of GDP (2013 est.)

country comparison to the world: 160

Inflation rate (consumer prices):

6.8% (2013 est.)

country comparison to the world: 183

2.7% (2012 est.)

Central bank discount rate:

13.73% (22 December 2011 est.)

country comparison to the world: 110

2.5% (31 December 2010 est.)

Commercial bank prime lending rate:

25% (31 December 2013 est.)

country comparison to the world: 7

28.43% (31 December 2012 est.)

Stock of narrow money:

$1.479 billion (31 December 2013 est.)

country comparison to the world: 140

$1.372 billion (31 December 2012 est.)

Stock of broad money:

$1.776 billion (31 December 2013 est.)

country comparison to the world: 155

$1.634 billion (31 December 2012 est.)

Stock of domestic credit:

$1.011 billion (31 December 2013 est.)

country comparison to the world: 154

$932.5 million (31 December 2012 est.)

Market value of publicly traded shares:

$165 million (31 December 2012 est.)

country comparison to the world: 117

$165 million (31 December 2011)

$79 million (31 December 2010 est.)

Current account balance:

-$1.125 billion (2013 est.)

country comparison to the world: 122

-$1.497 billion (2012 est.)

Exports:

$1.881 billion (2013 est.)

country comparison to the world: 142

$1.921 billion (2012 est.)

Exports - commodities:

gold, cotton, wool, garments, meat, tobacco; mercury, uranium, electricity; machinery; shoes

Exports - partners:

Kazakhstan 26.2%, Uzbekistan 26.1%, Russia 14.6%, China 7%, UAE 6.1%, Afghanistan 5.2% (2012)

Imports:

$5.082 billion (2013 est.)

country comparison to the world: 127

$4.967 billion (2012 est.)

Imports - commodities:

oil and gas, machinery and equipment, chemicals, foodstuffs

Imports - partners:

China 55.2%, Russia 17.4%, Kazakhstan 7.9% (2012)

Reserves of foreign exchange and gold:

$2.199 billion (31 December 2013 est.)

country comparison to the world: 120

$2.066 billion (31 December 2012 est.)

Debt - external:

$3.859 billion (31 December 2013 est.)

country comparison to the world: 129

$3.746 billion (31 December 2012 est.)

Stock of direct foreign investment – at home:

$2.005 billion (31 December 2013 est.)

country comparison to the world: 98

1.685 billion (31 December 2012 est.)

Stock of direct foreign investment – abroad:

$39.6 million (31 December 2013 est.)

country comparison to the world: 90

39.6 million (31 December 2012 est.)

Exchange rates:

soms (KGS) per US dollar -

48.87 (2013 est.)

47.005 (2012 est.)

45.964 (2010 est.)

42.905 (2009)

36.108 (2008)

Chapter 6: Energy

Electricity - production:

14.9 billion kWh (2011 est.)

country comparison to the world: 82

Electricity - consumption:

7.326 billion kWh (2010 est.)

country comparison to the world: 98

Electricity - exports:

2.62 billion kWh (2011 est.)

country comparison to the world: 38

Electricity - imports:

0 kWh (2010 est.)

country comparison to the world: 160

Electricity - installed generating capacity:

3.64 million kW (2010 est.)

country comparison to the world: 83

Electricity - from fossil fuels:

20.1% of total installed capacity (2010 est.)

country comparison to the world: 191

Electricity - from nuclear fuels:

0% of total installed capacity (2010 est.)

country comparison to the world: 117

Electricity - from hydroelectric plants:

79.9% of total installed capacity (2010 est.)

country comparison to the world: 15

Electricity - from other renewable sources:

0% of total installed capacity (2010 est.)

country comparison to the world: 186

Crude oil - production:

1,000 bbl/day (2011 est.)

country comparison to the world: 109

Crude oil - exports:

0 bbl/day (2010 est.)

country comparison to the world: 136

Crude oil - imports:

0 bbl/day (2010 est.)

country comparison to the world: 203

Crude oil - proved reserves:

40 million bbl (1 January 2013 es)

country comparison to the world: 80

Refined petroleum products - production:

0 bbl/day (2010 est.)

country comparison to the world: 158

Refined petroleum products - consumption:

16,640 bbl/day (2011 est.)

country comparison to the world: 139

Refined petroleum products - exports:

2,433 bbl/day (2010 est.)

country comparison to the world: 99

Refined petroleum products - imports:

35,040 bbl/day (2010 est.)

country comparison to the world:86

Natural gas - production:

10 million cu m (2011 est.)

country comparison to the world: 90

Natural gas - consumption:

462.5 million cu m (2010 est.)

country comparison to the world: 98

Natural gas - exports:

0 cu m (2011 est.)

country comparison to the world: 127

Natural gas - imports:

390 million cu m (2011 est.)

country comparison to the world: 66

Natural gas - proved reserves:

5.663 billion cu m (1 January 2013 es)

country comparison to the world: 94

Carbon dioxide emissions from consumption of energy:

7.793 million Mt (2011 est.)

country comparison to the world: 110

Chapter 7: Communications

Telephones - main lines in use:

489,000 (2012)

country comparison to the world: 98

Telephones - mobile cellular:

6.8 million (2012)

country comparison to the world: 94

Telephone system:

general assessment: telecommunications infrastructure is being upgraded; loans from the European Bank for Reconstruction and Development (EBRD) are being used to install a digital network, digital radio-relay stations, and fiber-optic links

domestic: fixed-line penetration remains low and concentrated in urban areas; multiple mobile-cellular service providers with growing coverage; mobile-cellular subscribership was about 115 per 100 persons in 2011

international: country code - 996; connections with other CIS countries by landline or microwave radio relay and with other countries by leased connections with Moscow international gateway switch and by satellite; satellite earth stations - 2 (1 Intersputnik, 1 Intelsat); connected internationally by the Trans-Asia-Europe (TAE) fiber-optic line (2011)

Broadcast media:

state-run TV broadcaster operates 2 nationwide networks and 6 regional stations; roughly 20 private TV stations operating with most rebroadcasting other channels; state-run radio broadcaster operates 2 networks; about 20 private radio stations (2007)

Internet country code:

.kg

Internet hosts:

115,573 (2012)

country comparison to the world: 81

Internet users:

2.195 million (2009)

country comparison to the world: 74

Chapter 8: Transportation

Airports:

>28 (2013)

>country comparison to the world: 122

Airports - with paved runways:

>total: 18

>over 3,047 m: 1

>2,438 to 3,047 m: 3

>1,524 to 2,437 m: 11

>under 914 m: 3 (2013)

Airports - with unpaved runways:

>total: 10

>1,524 to 2,437 m: 1

>914 to 1,523 m: 1

>under 914 m: 8 (2013)

Pipelines:

>gas 480 km; oil 16 km (2013)

Railways:

>total: 470 km

>country comparison to the world: 112

>broad gauge: 470 km 1.520-m gauge (2008)

Roadways:

>total: 34,000 km (2007)

>country comparison to the world: 94

Waterways:

600 km (2010)

<u>country comparison to the world:</u> 79

Ports and terminals:

<u>lake port(s):</u> Balykchy (Ysyk-Kol or Rybach'ye) (Lake Ysyk-Kol)

Chapter 9: Military

Military branches:

> Ground Forces, Air Force (includes Air Defense Forces) (2013)

Military service age and obligation:

> 18-27 years of age for compulsory or voluntary male military service in the Armed Forces or Interior Ministry; service obligation - 1 year, with optional fee-based 3-year service in the callup mobilization reserve; women may volunteer at age 19; 16-17 years of age for military cadets, who cannot take part in military operations (2013)

Manpower available for military service:

> males age 16-49: 1,456,881
>
> females age 16-49: 1,470,317 (2010 est.)

Manpower fit for military service:

> males age 16-49: 1,119,224
>
> females age 16-49: 1,257,263 (2010 est.)

Manpower reaching militarily significant age annually:

> male: 56,606
>
> female: 54,056 (2010 est.)

Military expenditures:

> NA% (2012)
>
> 3.74% of GDP (2011)
>
> NA% (2010)

Chapter 10: Transnational Issues

Disputes - international:

Kyrgyzstan has yet to ratify the 2001 boundary delimitation with Kazakhstan; disputes in Isfara Valley delay completion of delimitation with Tajikistan; delimitation of 130 km of border with Uzbekistan is hampered by serious disputes over enclaves and other areas

Refugees and internally displaced persons:

IDPs: 172,000 (June 2010 violence in southern Kyrgyzstan between the Kyrgyz majority and the Uzbek minority) (2012)

stateless persons: 15,473 (2012); note - most stateless people were born in Kyrgystan, have lived there many years, or are married to a Kyrgyz citizen; in 2009, Kyrgyzstan adopted a national action plan to speed up the exchange of old Soviet passports for Kyrgyz ones; stateless people are unable to register marriages and births, to travel within the country or abroad, to own property, or to receive social benefits

Illicit drugs:

limited illicit cultivation of cannabis and opium poppy for CIS markets; limited government eradication of illicit crops; transit point for Southwest Asian narcotics bound for Russia and the rest of Europe; major consumer of opiates

Map of Kyrgyzstan

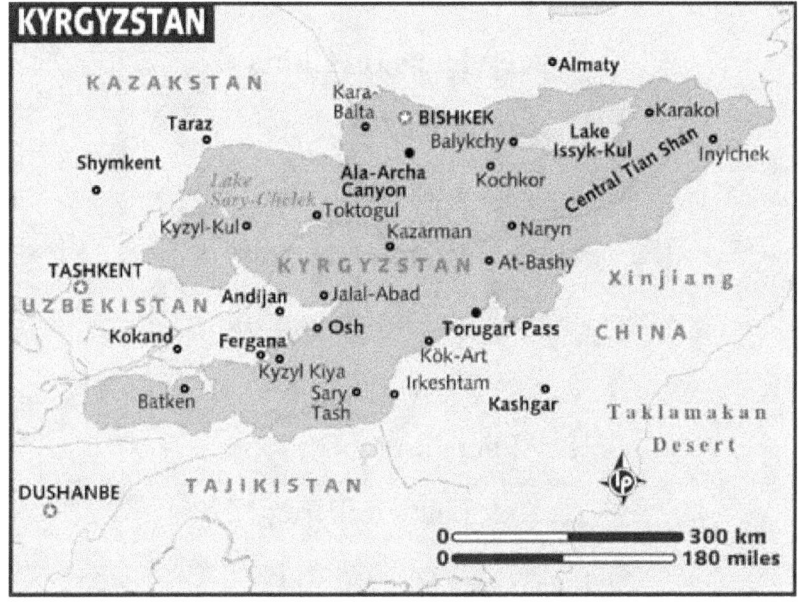

Other Key Facts™ Titles

Key Facts on South Korea

Key Facts on France

Key Facts on the United Kingdom

Key Facts on Egypt

Key Facts on Israel

All Key Facts™ Titles are Available at

www.Amazon.com

THE INTERNATIONALIST®

2014

WWW.INTERNATIONALIST.COM